EASTER

Philip Sauvain

WAYLAND

CARNIVAL

CHINESE NEW YEAR

CHRISTMAS

DIWALI

EASTER

ID-UL-FITR

PASSOVER

Series editor: Sarah Doughty
Book editor: Merle Thompson
Designer: Tim Mayer

First published in 1997 by Wayland Publishers Ltd
61 Western Road, Hove, East Sussex BN3 1JD

Find Wayland on the Internet at http://www.wayland.co.uk

British Library Cataloguing in Publication Data
Sauvain, Philip,
Easter. – (Festivals)
1. Easter – Juvenile literature
1. Title
394.2'68283

ISBN 0 7502 2120 8

Printed and bound by Eurografica, Italy

Picture acknowledgements
AKG 6, 7 top, 8, 16 top; The Bridgeman Art Library 7 bottom; Britstock 10, 13, 22, 27 bottom; Chapel Studios (Zul Mukhida) 20; Chris Fairclough 17; J Allan Cash 15; Sonia Halliday 24; Robert Harding 5 right; Impact cover top right; Magnum 5 left, 23; St Albans and Harpenden Observer 4 top; Tony Stone cover middle, 12, 16 bottom (James Davis), 18 bottom, 26, 28; Trip 4 middle, bottom left and right, 11, 14, 18 top, 21 top, 25, 27 top, 29; Zefa cover top left, bottom middle and left, title page, 19, 21.
Border artwork by Tim Mayer.

CONTENTS

EASTER AROUND THE WORLD

Easter Monday is a holiday in many countries. Christians celebrate in many ways. Every Easter Monday some Christians make a special pilgrimage to local churches. This is St Albans Abbey in Hertfordshire, Britain. Groups from many local churches set out early to walk to the abbey for a special service.

An Easter Vigil Service in Romania. People in the congregation stream out of the church carrying their candles to greet the start of Easter Sunday.

Children at a Palm Sunday Service in Benin, West Africa. Palm crosses are given out to the congregation on this day. This is because, when Jesus rode into Jerusalem, people welcomed him by waving palm branches.

On Good Friday, in Jerusalem, Christians carry a wooden cross through the streets. They follow the path taken by Jesus on his way to Golgotha, the place of Crucifixion. The path through the narrow streets is called the Via Dolorosa, or the 'Road of Sorrows'.

An Easter Sunday service in Washington DC, America.

Palm Sunday celebrations in Peru, South America. In many parts of the world, Christians act out the events of Jesus' life throughout Holy Week. They take part in what is really a long Passion play. Here, Christians in Peru are acting out Jesus' entry into Jerusalem. Sometimes Jesus is represented, as here, by a statue.

THE EASTER STORY

Easter is the most important time of the year for Christians. In Holy Week they remember the last week in the life of Jesus Christ which ended with his death. On Easter Day they celebrate Jesus rising from the dead – the Resurrection.

This picture, painted by Christians many years ago, shows Jesus riding on a donkey into Jerusalem at the time of the Passover. His right hand is raised to bless the crowd.

The events that Christians remember at Easter can be found in the New Testament. Christians read about them in the Gospels according to St Matthew, St Mark, St Luke and St John. Jesus lived over 2,000 years ago in the part of the world then known as Palestine. At that time it was part of the Roman Empire. Many of the people who lived there were Jews. Some believed that Jesus was the Messiah, the hoped-for leader who would save the Jews. This is why a large crowd greeted Jesus when he went to Jerusalem at the time of the Jewish festival of the Passover. People threw palm branches in front of him, shouting 'Hosanna'. The Gospel stories tell how Jesus was betrayed to the authorities by Judas Iscariot, one of his close followers or disciples. The chief priests agreed to pay Judas thirty pieces of silver for doing this.

At Jesus' last meal with his disciples, he told them how they were to remember him. St Matthew's Gospel says that Jesus blessed bread and gave it to the disciples. He said, 'Take this and eat; this is my body.' He then took the cup of wine. After he had blessed it, he gave it to the disciples and said, 'Drink from it, all of you. For this is my blood.' Christians call this last meal The Last Supper.

On the next day Jesus was arrested, and taken before the Roman Governor of Palestine, Pontius Pilate. The artist who carved this scene in stone, showed Pontius Pilate sitting on the left. Jesus was sentenced to death.

GOSPELS

The first Christians made many beautiful copies of the Gospels and decorated them with pictures.

In this copy of the Gospels, the artist has drawn a picture of St Mark turning over the pages of a book on a reading desk.

Jesus was sentenced to be crucified. This was a very cruel way of punishing people. They were fixed to a wooden cross and left to die. According to the stories in the Gospels, Jesus was nailed to the Cross at 9 am in the morning. After much suffering, he died at 3 pm in the afternoon. Towards evening, his body was wrapped in cloth and later placed in a tomb. A large stone was rolled across to block the entrance to the tomb and Roman soldiers stood on guard outside.

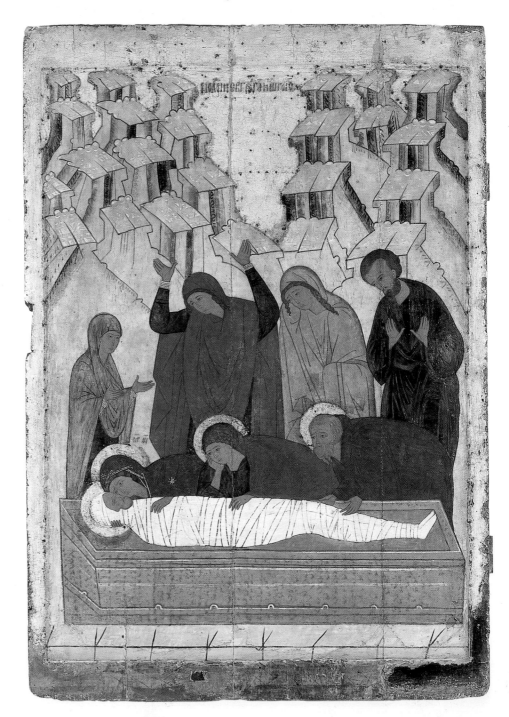

This is how an artist painted Jesus' body after it was taken down from the Cross and wrapped in cloth. The picture also shows Mary, Jesus' mother, and other disciples weeping over his body.

St Mark's Gospel tells us that Mary Magdalene and two other women went to the tomb at sunrise on the first day of the new week. They were very upset to see the stone had been moved. The tomb was empty.

St Mark then says that, later that morning, Mary Magdalene saw Jesus. But when she told other people whom she had seen, no one believed her.

The Church of the Holy Sepulchre in Jerusalem. Christians later built this Church on the site where they thought Jesus' body had been buried.

After this, Jesus met the disciples as well. He told them to go out into the world to preach the gospel. St Mark writes: 'So after talking with them, the Lord Jesus was taken up into heaven'.

THE RESURRECTION

The Gospel stories tell us that, after Mary Magdalene saw the risen Jesus, the other disciples saw him too. Jesus met with them and spoke with them several times. St Mark says that Jesus' last words to his disciples were: 'I am with you always'. The disciples were overjoyed. Today Christians celebrate the Resurrection on Easter Sunday. They, too, are joyful because they believe that Jesus overcame death.

EASTER TODAY

Long before Jesus was born, some people worshipped a goddess of Spring called Eostre. Many think this is how Easter got its name.

Others say it comes from the word East – the direction from which the Christian religion came to Europe.

Unlike Christmas, Easter Sunday is always celebrated on a different day from year to year. It might be in April one year and in March the next. Christians decided, many years ago, that Easter Sunday should always be the first Sunday after the first full moon that appears, following the first day of Spring on 21 March. This is why Easter is called a movable feast.

When Christians think of Spring, they think of Easter as well. These lambs remind them that Easter, too, is about new life – about Jesus rising from the dead.

The period of forty days before Easter is called Lent. At one time, all Christians used to fast during Lent. They would not eat rich foods, such as fats, meat and eggs. This is because Jesus once spent forty days fasting in the wilderness.

Some Christians still fast today and many will go without luxuries, such as sweets or chocolate, during Lent. Many will spend more time praying and reading the Bible. They ask God's forgiveness for their sins and help people in need.

Christians celebrating the dawning of Easter Day in Romania. The Eastern Churches use a different method of working out the date of Easter from the Western Churches. Their Easter Sunday is usually about a week or so later than Easter Sunday in the West.

ASH WEDNESDAY

Ash Wednesday, the first day of Lent, gets its name from the ash that is placed on the foreheads of people in church. Ash is a sign that people are sorry for their sins. It reminds them that everyone turns to dust in the end.

SHROVE TUESDAY

Because Lent is a solemn time of prayer and fasting, Christians in the past made sure they had a good time on Shrove Tuesday, the day before it begins. They ate all the foods that they would give up during Lent. Many of these Shrovetide customs are still carried on today.

Colourful carnival masks for sale in a shop window in Venice.

In Italy, the people of Venice hold a carnival each year. It lasts ten days and ends on Shrove Tuesday with a grand ball and dancing in the streets. Women wear elaborate dresses and men put on black hats and cloaks.

MARDI GRAS

In France, Shrove Tuesday is called Mardi Gras. This means 'Fat Tuesday' or 'Greasy Tuesday'. The best-known Mardi Gras festival is the one in New Orleans in America. It is famous for its jazz bands, fancy dress and huge decorated floats.

South America is also famous for its carnivals. This one in Rio de Janeiro lasts for several days before ending on Shrove Tuesday. The people of Brazil who take part in the Carnival wear bright and colourful clothes covered in feathers and sequins. There are prizes for the best costumes and many cost a lot of money to make. People sing and dance the samba as they ride through the city on huge floats.

PANCAKES

Long ago, people in Britain made pancakes on Shrove Tuesday to use up all the cooking fat in the house before the start of Lent. Pancakes are still made today from a batter made from eggs, flour and milk. They are cooked in a frying pan. When one side is ready, the pancake is tossed in the air and turned over. At Olney, near London, women from the village race against each other to see who can reach the church first. They have to toss a pancake three times without dropping it in order to win.

HOLY WEEK

Holy Week is the last week of Lent. This is the most solemn time of the year for Christians. The events of this week act out the last days of Jesus' life. They end with the Passion – the suffering – of Jesus on the Cross.

Children with palm crosses at a Palm Sunday service in Benin, West Africa.

The week begins with Palm Sunday. To celebrate Jesus' entry into Jerusalem, processions are held in many towns. Palm crosses made of leaves are given to people who go to church. Since palm trees only grow in hot places, willow trees, or branches of blossom from a fruit tree, are often used instead.

Every time Christians celebrate Holy Communion they remember the Last Supper. This service is held every Sunday and on many other days throughout the year.

Christians share bread and wine like the disciples did on Maundy Thursday. But, on the Thursday of Holy Week, Christians especially remember the events of that day, and the way in which Judas betrayed Jesus.

On Maundy Thursday, Christians also remember some of the other things Jesus did on that evening. St John's Gospel tells how Jesus washed the disciples feet and told them, 'I have set you an example: you are to do as I have done for you'.

Even British rulers used to wash the feet of twelve poor people every Maundy Thursday until about 350 years ago. Then the ceremony was changed. Instead of washing feet, the king or queen made a gift of Maundy money to old people in need.

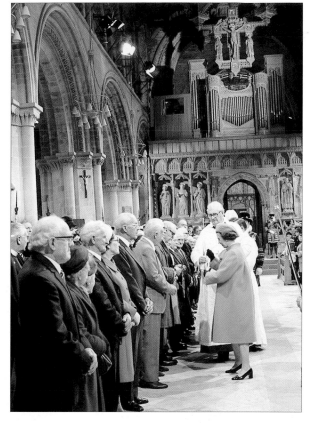

The Maundy money ceremony is still held today in Britain. The Queen gives a gift of Maundy money to one man and one woman for each year of her life. Here the service is being held at St David's Cathedral in Wales.

THE FLIGHT OF THE BELLS

Church bells ring out for the last time on Maundy Thursday. Then they remain silent until Easter Sunday. In France, Roman Catholic children are sometimes told that the bells have flown to Rome to see the Pope. When the bells return again on Sunday, they will bring Easter eggs for all the children.

GOOD FRIDAY

Since the time of the first Christians, many thousands of artists have painted the Crucifixion scene in different ways. This is how the artist, Paul Gauguin, painted Jesus on the Cross about a hundred years ago.

Good Friday means God's Friday. It is a day of sorrow and prayer. Christians are sorrowful when they remember the time when Jesus died on the Cross. A cross has become the sign of a Christian. Christians often wear a cross on a chain. Hot cross buns have a cross on top. Many churches when seen from the air are shaped like a cross.

Because Good Friday is a day of mourning, some Christians fast all day or eat only a little food. Many eat fish instead of meat. Church services often start at midday on Good Friday and last until 3 pm because this was the time when Jesus died on the Cross.

Right: Christians at a service on Good Friday in a church in Greece. Here Christians decorate a 'tomb' to represent the place where Jesus was buried and put it in the middle of the church. Often it is decorated with flowers.

The Crucifixion is remembered in Jerusalem today by large crowds of Christians who walk in the steps taken by Jesus. They stop at the fourteen Stations of the Cross to pray at the places connected with the Crucifixion. In some countries, such as Spain and the Philippines, people act out the story of Jesus' last hours. Volunteers play the part of Jesus, Judas and the Romans. People in the watching crowds imagine they are taking part in events which happened long ago.

AN EASTER GARDEN

In many parts of Europe, children make an Easter Garden or grotto. This is a model of the garden where Jesus was laid to rest. They use a stone to show the tomb where Jesus was buried.

An Easter Garden in a British church with figures of the risen Jesus, and Mary Magdalene kneeling before him. A small stone has been put in the garden to represent Jesus' tomb.

HAPPY EASTER

The lighting of the Easter candle or, as it is often called, 'the holy fire'. Soon this church in Eastern Europe will blaze with light.

After the sorrow of Good Friday, Easter Sunday is the happiest time of the year. This is when Christians celebrate the Resurrection. People long ago believed that if you got up very early in the morning, you could even see the sun dancing to celebrate the start of Easter Day.

Many Christians keep a vigil in church on Saturday night. They wait in darkness to greet the start of Easter Day. Then the priest lights a special Easter candle – the Paschal candle – at midnight. This candle is then used to light the candles held by the people. Sometimes the light for the candle comes from a fire outside the church and sometimes fireworks are let off after the service to show that everyone is happy.

St Peter's Square in Rome, Italy. Every Easter the Pope steps on to the balcony to give his Easter Blessing to the huge crowd waiting below. Nowadays, this ceremony is watched on television across the world.

Because it is a day of great joy, the church bells ring out once more. People eat their favourite foods again. Two hundred years ago, people in Ireland used to put a chicken in the pot on the Saturday night. They made sure it was ready to eat as soon as the clocks struck midnight. Many other old customs used to be followed on Easter Day. One of these was the Easter Laugh. The priest told the people in church stories to make them laugh after all the sorrow of Good Friday and the weeks of fasting during Lent.

A boy carries a candle at an Easter Day procession outside the Church of the Holy Sepulchre in Jerusalem.

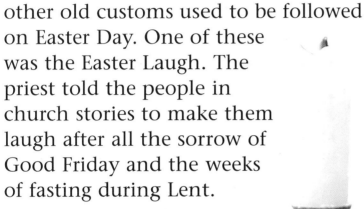

THE EASTER FLOWER

The white lily is the special Easter flower. White is a sign of purity. Easter lilies are used to decorate many churches at this time.

EGG SUNDAY

There are many Easter customs that involve eggs. Some take place on Easter Day. This is why it used to be called Egg Sunday. Since no one could eat eggs during Lent, there were always lots left over by then. Children in many countries today are still given hard-boiled eggs as a treat on Easter Day. In Britain, they usually get chocolate eggs instead.

In America and in Europe, parents hide eggs in the garden or in the house for the children to find.

Children enjoy hunting for chocolate eggs that have been hidden in the garden on Easter Day.

Easter Sunday is also a time for making gifts as well as for receiving presents. Eliza and Mary Chaulkhurst were twin sisters who lived in the English village of Biddenden hundreds of years ago. When they died, they left a plot of land – the Bread and Cheese Lands – to the village. In future, the rent from the land would be used to buy bread and cheese and be given to the poor people of the village on Easter Sunday. The gifts of bread and cheese donated by Mary and Eliza Chaulkhurst are still made today hundreds of years after they died. Spectators at the ceremony are given special biscuits, called Biddenden Cakes.

Children, in many countries, decorate hard-boiled eggs for Easter by painting or dyeing them in bright colours. Here a young girl is rubbing the eggs with olive oil to make them shine, after they have been dyed red. In some countries these eggs are called Peace Eggs, Paste Eggs or Pace Eggs. All these names come from the Hebrew word Pesach which means Passover.

EGGS

The egg is a sign of hope and the Resurrection of Jesus. This is because of the way in which the chick breaks from the egg at birth.

A basket of brightly coloured eggs.

EASTER MONDAY

Easter Monday is a holiday in many countries. In Hungary, it used to be called Ducking Monday because young men ducked their girl friends in a pond or river. Nowadays they splash them with water instead. At one time in Britain, it was called Ball Monday because people played ball games then, sometimes in church.

On Easter Monday, the American President invites children to roll eggs on the lawn of the White House in Washington DC. The winners are those whose eggs are still unbroken at the end of the day.

Egg-rolling is another favourite Easter Monday custom in many parts of the world, such as Scotland and Switzerland. The brightly coloured hard-boiled eggs are rolled down a slope. When they break, the owners eat the egg inside.

Egg-shackling is another Easter Monday sport. People taking part bang their hard-boiled eggs together. The winner keeps all the eggs he or she cracks until he loses his or her own. The Easter Egg Fights ceremony is held each year at Sugar Hill in the American state of North Carolina.

A GOLD EASTER EGG

Easter eggs can be very valuable. Many years ago, a Russian jeweller called Peter Fabergé made many beautiful eggs of solid gold, decorated with precious jewels. They were given by the Tsar, the ruler of Russia, to his wife and to other members of the royal family.

This beautiful Easter egg was made by the Russian jeweller Peter Fabergé for the Tsarina of Russia. A few years ago, an Easter egg like this was sold for nearly three million dollars (about two million pounds).

Some of the old Easter customs, such as lifting or heaving, have died out. This was a popular custom in many parts of England and Wales. Strangers were lifted up and not put down again until they gave money to a needy cause. The lifters who went out on Heaving Monday sometimes sang 'Jesus Christ is risen again!'

EASTER PLAYS AND PICTURES

Five hundred years ago, very few people could read the Bible for themselves. But, besides the Easter stories that the priest would tell them, they learnt about these events from paintings and carvings decorating the church. Many churches had brightly-coloured wall paintings, wood carvings, stone sculptures and stained glass windows showing the events of Holy week and Easter Day.

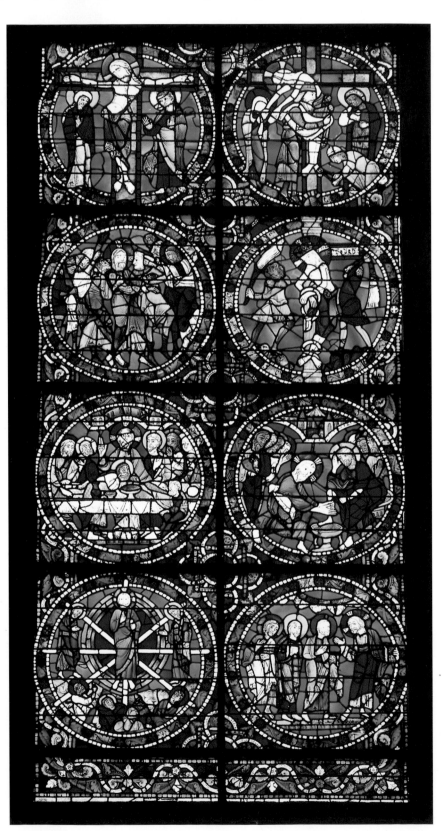

This stained glass window shows scenes from the Passion story. It was made by French craftsmen about eight hundred years ago and can be seen in the Cathedral of Chartres in France. The Crucifixion is shown at the top of the picture.

People also learned about the Easter Story from Passion plays. These were scenes from the Bible, such as the Last Supper. They were acted by local people. Passion plays are still performed today. In America you can see them at Strasburg in Virginia, Eureka Springs in Arizona and at Spearfish in the Black Hills of South Dakota.

OBERAMMERGAU

The most famous Passion play is the one put on by the people who live in the village of Oberammergau in Germany. Over 350 years ago, the people were suffering from a terrible disease called the Plague. They decided to put on a play about the Passion if God would save them from the Plague. When the disease went away they kept their promise. Their play is so famous, a special theatre was built for it, even though you can only see it once every ten years.

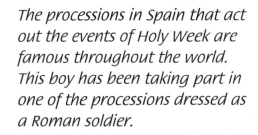

The processions in Spain that act out the events of Holy Week are famous throughout the world. This boy has been taking part in one of the processions dressed as a Roman soldier.

EASTER FOOD

Easter is a time for eating favourite types of food. Italians eat pretzels, a kind of salty biscuit. People in Denmark eat Shrovetide buns. Russians eat blini. These are pancakes covered in butter which are eaten during Butter Week, the last seven days before Lent. They also enjoy buns shaped like birds that have currants for their eyes.

Hot cross buns.

People in Britain eat hot cross buns at Easter. Many years ago these were baked very early in the morning and given away in church to poor people to be eaten for breakfast on Good Friday. They are called hot partly because they are filled with spices, and partly because they are always served hot from the oven. In the past hot cross buns were cheap. Traders sold them in the streets of London, singing a rhyme.

One a penny, buns!
Two a penny, buns!
One a penny, two a penny,
Hot Cross Buns!

Simnel cake is also eaten on Easter Day. The word simnel means 'the finest flour'. There are eleven knobs of almond paste on the top of the cake, one for each disciple (except for Judas).

Simnel cake is eaten on Mothering Sunday in the middle of Lent, as well as at Easter. Servant girls were allowed to go home to see their mothers on this day. They sometimes took a simnel cake with them as a present.

PASSION FRUIT

The Passion Fruit got its name from its flower. Europeans, who saw the plant in South America, said the flower reminded them of the Crucifixion and the Cross. One part of the flower looks like the nails used to crucify Jesus and another looks like the crown of thorns that the Roman soldiers put on his head.

A flower of the passion fruit plant.

THE CHRISTIAN CALENDAR

Advent December

The Christian Church begins its year in December with the season of Advent. It lasts just over three weeks and it is the time when people prepare for Christmas. Many children have Advent calendars which have 24 or 25 windows to open. They open a window each day to see the picture inside.

Christmas December

Christmas is the festival when Jesus Christ's birth is celebrated. It lasts for 12 days. Christmas Day is on 25 December, although Orthodox Christians celebrate Christmas on 6 January.

Epiphany 6 January

Epiphany is the last of the 12 days of Christmas. Epiphany means 'showing', and it celebrates the story of Jesus being shown to the wise men who had travelled to see the new baby king.

Shrove Tuesday

This is the day before the beginning of Lent. It is also known as Pancake Day. People used to make pancakes to use up foods such as fat and eggs that would go off during Lent, when everyone was fasting. Shrove Tuesday is known in many countries by its French name, Mardi Gras, which means 'Fat Tuesday'. It is celebrated with a carnival that sometimes lasts for a week.

Lent Spring

Lent takes place during the six weeks before Easter. It is the time when Christians feel sorry for anything they have done wrong and try to make a new start in their lives. It used to be a time for fasting, and many people still give up something they enjoy during Lent.

Good Friday March or April
Good Friday is a very solemn day when Christians remember that Jesus died on the Cross.

Easter Sunday March or April
Easter is when Christians celebrate Jesus' rising from the dead. In many countries, eggs are eaten because they are a symbol of new life. In the Orthodox Church, services are held at midnight as Easter Day begins. The dark church is gradually filled with lighted candles as a symbol that the 'Light of the World' has returned.

Ascension Day May
Ascension Day is forty days after Easter. It is the day when Jesus was last seen on Earth.

Pentecost
The Day of Pentecost was the time when Jesus' disciples were given the power of the Holy Spirit to guide them in their work of telling everyone about God. Many Christians hold processions on this day. It is also known as Whit Sunday.

Harvest Festival
September or October
Churches are decorated with fruit, vegetables and sheaves of corn, as well as flowers, at harvest festival. It is a time when people thank God for the harvest and for providing them with food.

GLOSSARY

Christ The name given to Jesus by his followers. It comes from the Greek word 'Christos' meaning Messiah. This is why people who believe in Christ are called Christians.

Crucifixion The means by which the Romans put criminals and traitors to death. They were fastened to a cross until they died.

Fast To fast means to go without food. A fast means a period of days or weeks when people eat little or no food.

Golgotha The small hill outside Jerusalem where Jesus was crucified. It means 'the place of the skull'. The site of the Crucifixion is also called Calvary.

Gospel This means good news. It is used to describe an account of Jesus' life and work.

Jerusalem At one time, this city used to be the main city of Palestine. It is a holy city for Muslims and Jews as well as for Christians.

Maundy Thursday 'Maundy' is an old word meaning 'commandment'. Maundy Thursday got its name because this was when Jesus told his disciples to celebrate the Last Supper in remembrance of Him.

Messiah A Jewish word for the hoped-for leader from God, who would save the Jews.

Orthodox Church The Church to which Christians in Russia and many parts of Eastern Europe belong.

Palestine At the time of Jesus, Palestine was part of the Roman Empire. Christians sometimes refer to it as The Holy Land. Today it is partly in Israel and partly in Jordan.

Paschal This word comes from the Hebrew word 'Pesach' meaning the Passover. It is used to describe anything connected with Easter.

Passion The suffering of Jesus Christ, especially in the time leading up to his death on the Cross.

Passover This Jewish Festival, known to Jews as Pesach, is celebrated in the spring. Jews remember how God delivered them from the Egyptians over 3,000 years ago.

Roman Catholic Church The part of the Christian Church whose leader is the Pope in Rome, Italy.

Roman Empire At the time when Jesus was alive, the Romans ruled over Palestine. This is why Pontius Pilate, the Roman Governor, had the authority to pass a sentence of death on Jesus.

Vigil This means staying awake at night, keeping watch until dawn.

BOOKS TO READ

A Feast of Festivals by Hugo Slim (Marshall Pickering, 1996)

Celebrating Christian Festivals by Jan Thompson (Heinemann, 1995)

Christianity by John Logan (Wayland, 1995)

Christians by John Drane (Lion Publishing, 1994)

The Easter Book by Anne Farncombe (National Christian Education Council, 1983)

The Easter Story by Brian Wildsmith (Oxford, 1993)

The Easter Story by C. Rawson and the Revd R. H. Lloyd (Usborne, 1981)

USEFUL ADDRESSES

To find out more about Christianity, you may find these addresses useful:

The British Council of Churches, 2 Eaton Gate, London, SW1W 9BT.

Catholic Information Service, 74 Gallow Hill Lane, Abbotts Langley, Herts, WD5 OBZ.

Christian Education Movement, 2 Chester House, Pages Lane, London, N10 1PR.

Church of England Information Office, Church House, Deans Yard, London, N10, 1PR.

Committee for Extra-Diocesan Affairs, Russian Orthodox Cathedral, Ennismore Gardens, London SW7.

Society of Friends, Friends House, Euston Road, London, NW1 2BJ